PHILIPPE LEGENDRE

 KIDS CAN DRAW

# African Animals

Walter Foster Publishing, Inc.
23062 La Cadena Drive
Laguna Hills, CA 92653 USA
ISBN 1-56010-275-6

## Attention Parents and Teachers

All children can draw a circle, a square, or a triangle…which means that they can also learn to draw a lion, zebra, or hippopotamus! The KIDS CAN DRAW learning method is easy and fun. Children will learn a technique and a vocabulary of shapes that will form the basis for all kinds of drawing.

Pictures are created by combining geometric shapes to form a mass of volumes and surfaces. From this stage, children can give character to their sketches with straight, curved, or broken lines.

With just a few strokes of the pencil, an African animal will appear—and with the addition of color, the picture will be real work of art!

The KIDS CAN DRAW method offers a real apprenticeship in technique and a first look at composition, proportion, shapes, and lines. The simplicity of this method ensures that the pleasure of drawing is always the most important factor.

## About Philippe Legendre

French painter, engraver, and illustrator, Philippe Legendre also runs a school of art for children aged 6–14 years. Legendre frequently spends time in schools and has developed this method of learning so that all children can discover the artist within themselves.

# Helpful Tips

1. Each picture is made up of simple geometric shapes, which are illustrated at the top of the left-hand page. This is called the **Vocabulary of Shapes.** Encourage children to practice drawing each shape before starting their pictures.

2. Suggest children use a pencil to do their sketches. This way, if they don't like a particular shape, they can just erase it and try again.

3. A dotted line indicates that the line should be erased. Have children draw the whole shape and then erase the dotted part of the line.

4. Once children finish their drawings, they can color them with crayons, colored pencils, or felt-tip markers. They may want to go over the lines with a black pencil or pen.

## Now let's get started!

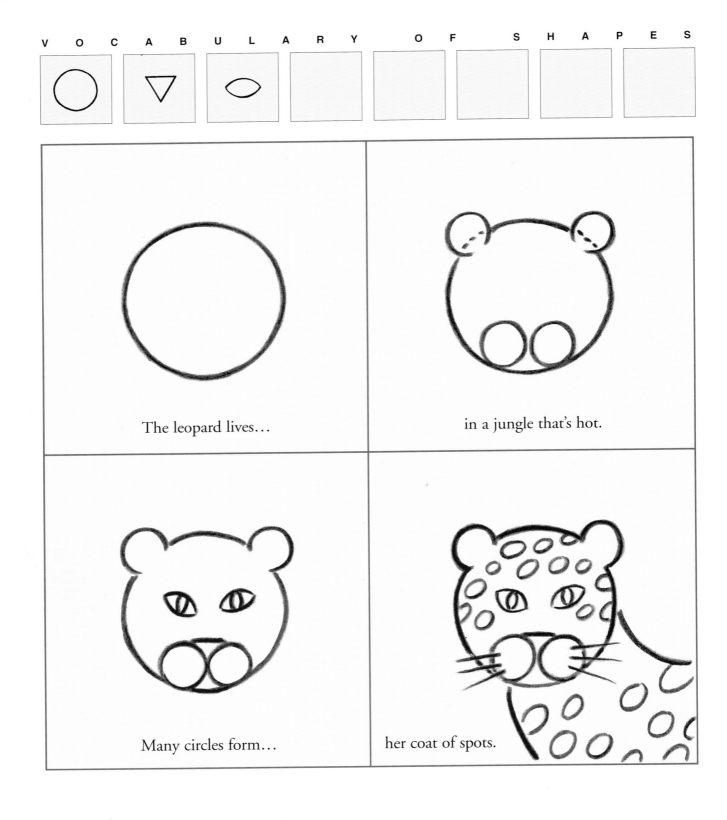

The leopard lives...

in a jungle that's hot.

Many circles form...

her coat of spots.

# Leopard

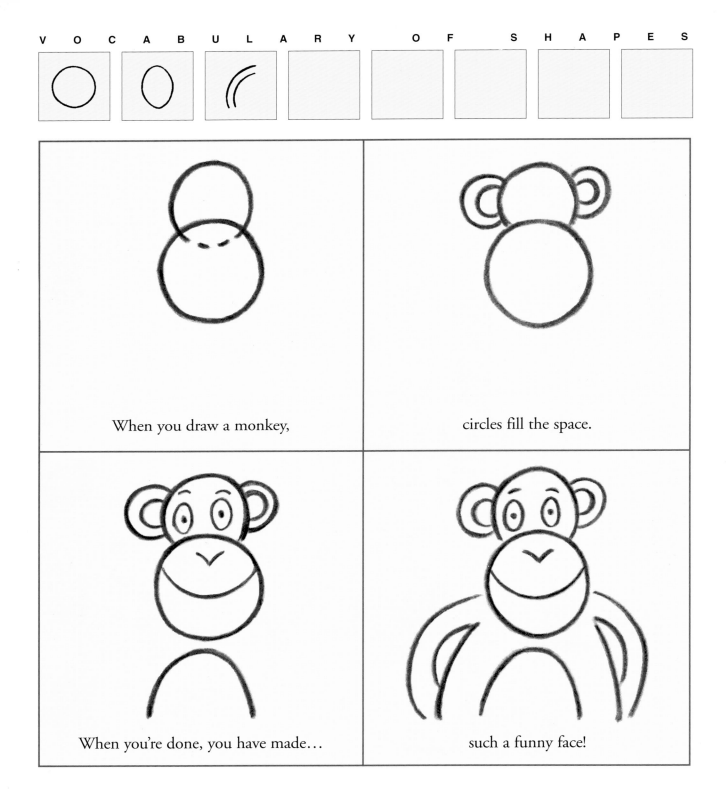

When you draw a monkey,

circles fill the space.

When you're done, you have made…

such a funny face!

# **M**onkey

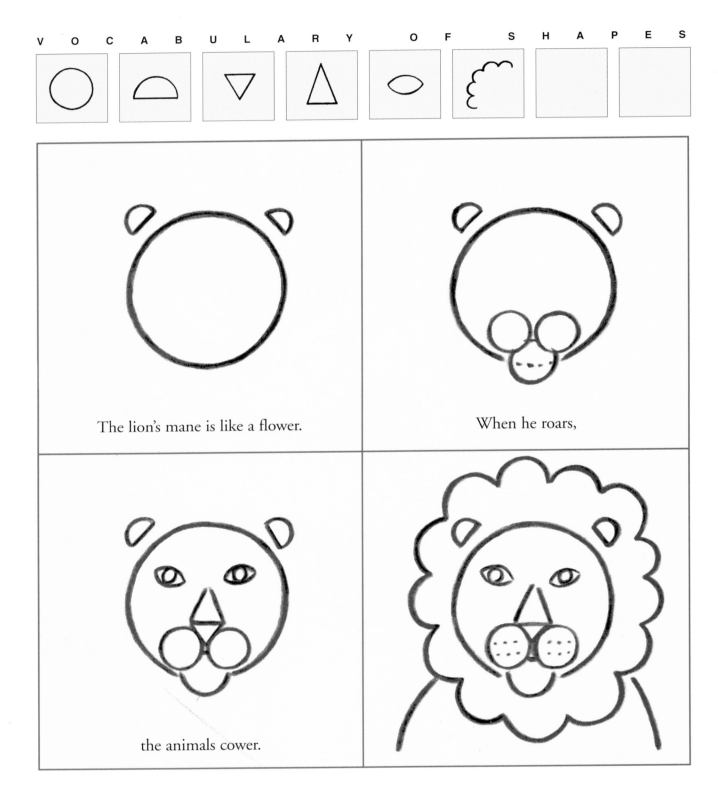

The lion's mane is like a flower.

When he roars,

the animals cower.

# Lion

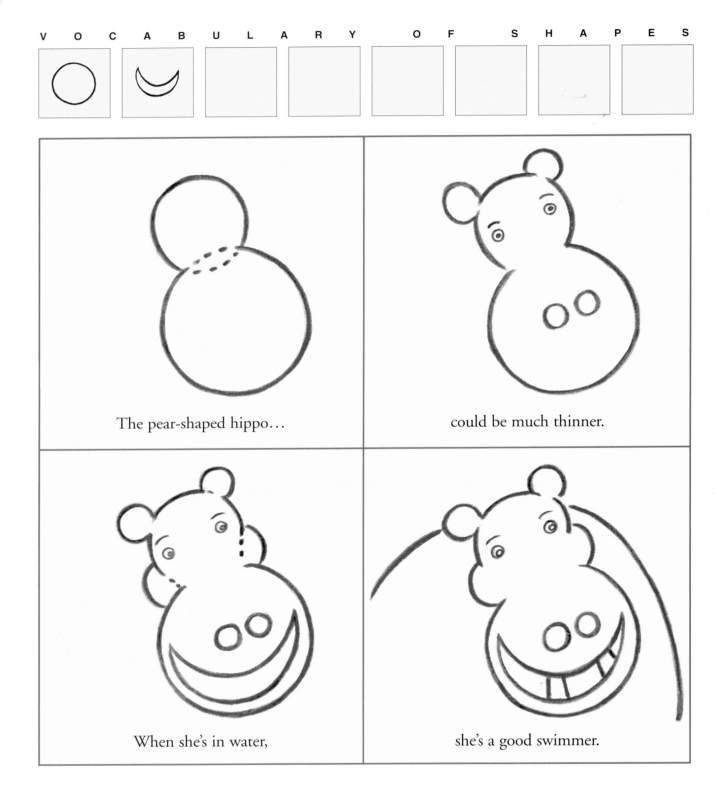

The pear-shaped hippo…

could be much thinner.

When she's in water,

she's a good swimmer.

# **H**ippopotamus

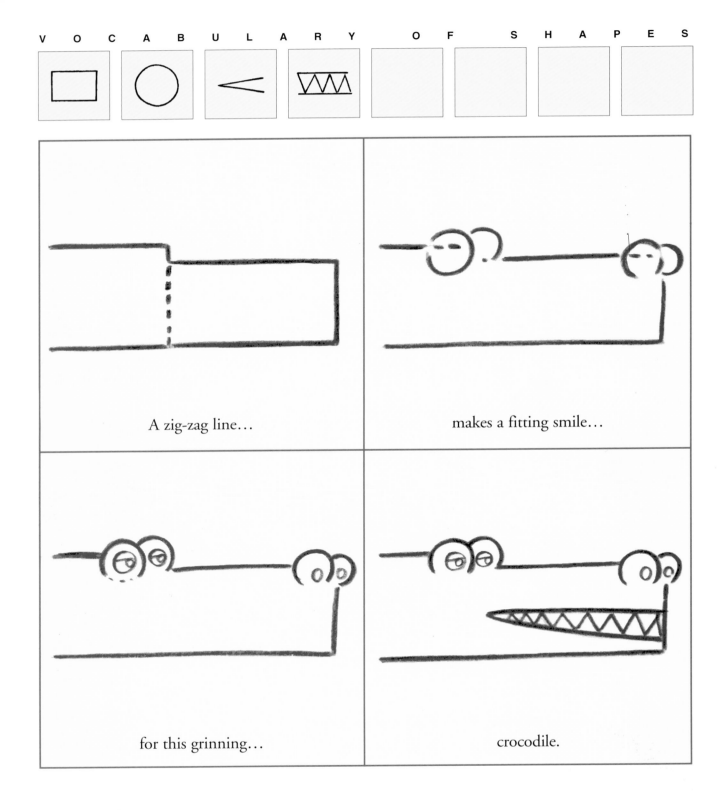

A zig-zag line…

makes a fitting smile…

for this grinning…

crocodile.

# Crocodile

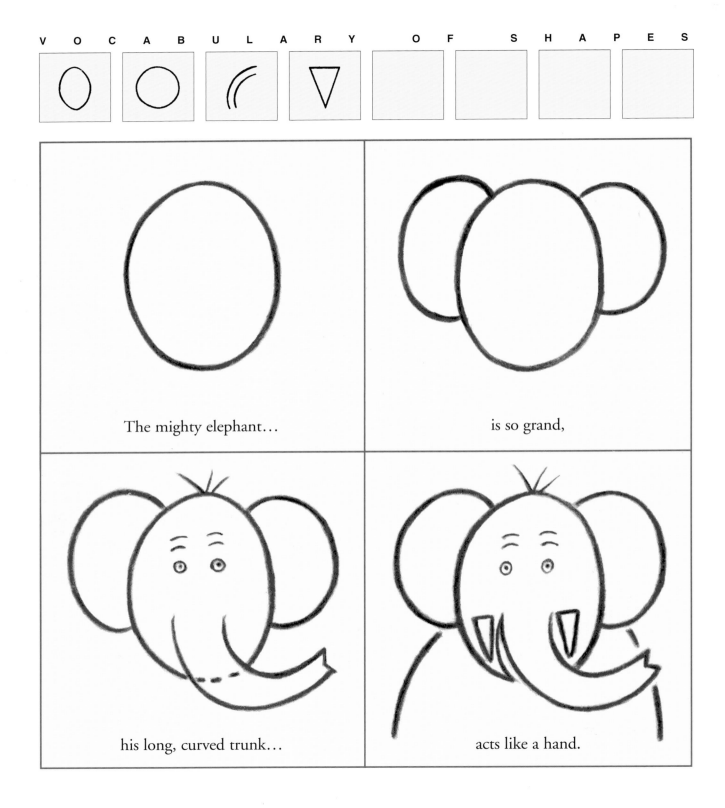

The mighty elephant…

is so grand,

his long, curved trunk…

acts like a hand.

# Elephant

Diamonds make the giraffe's ears...

and eyes so she can see.

Use a long line for her neck—

she's taller than a tree!

# Giraffe

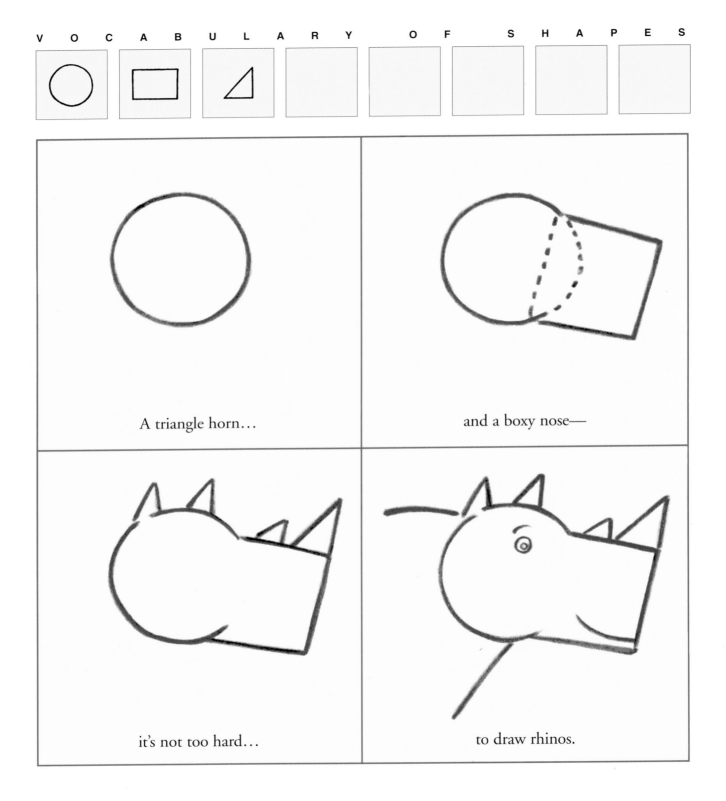

A triangle horn…

and a boxy nose—

it's not too hard…

to draw rhinos.

# **R**hinoceros

The zebra is quite a sight…

in black and white.

# Zebra

Now that you can draw these animals in pencil or ink,

add them to the riverbank sharing a peaceful drink.

| EI # | PRODUCT NAME |
|------|--------------|
| 4510 | Marker Mania/Art Start Kits |
| 4511 | Paint Pandemonium/Art Start Kits |
| 4512 | Papercraft & Origami/Mini Master Kits |
| 4513 | Printing/Mini Master Kits |
| 4514 | Optical Illusions/Mini Master Kits |
| 4515 | Magic/Mini Master Kits |
| 4516 | I Can Draw Books – Animals |
| 4517 | I Can Draw Books – Dinosaurs |
| 4518 | I Can Draw Books – Things That Move |
| 4519 | I Can Draw Books – Cartoons Animals |
| 4520 | I Can Draw Books – Cartoons |
| 4521 | I Can Draw Books – Creepy Creatures |
| 4522 | I Can Draw Books – Bugs |
| 4523 | I Can Draw Books – I Can Draw |
| 4524 | I Can Draw Books – Sea Creatures |
| 4525 | I Can Draw Books – Horses and Ponies |
| 4526 | Kids Can Draw – Arctic Animals |
| 4527 | Kids Can Draw – Forest Animals |
| 4528 | Kids Can Draw – Dinosaurs |
| 4529 | Kids Can Draw – Favorite Pets |
| 4530 | Kids Can Draw – The Ocean |
| 4531 | Kids Can Draw – The Mountains |
| 4532 | Kids Can Draw – African Animals |
| 4533 | Kids Can Draw – Animals of the World |
| 4534 | Kids Can Draw – Fairy Tales |
| 4535 | Kids Can Draw – The Circus |
| 4536 | Walter Foster Art Kits – Calligraphy Kit |
| 4537 | Crafts for Children – Face Painting |
| 4538 | Crafts for Children – Creative Crafts |
| 4539 | Crafts for Children – Papier Mache |

| EI # | PRODUCT NAME |
|------|--------------|
| 4540 | Crafts for Children – Children's Costumes |
| 4541 | Crafts for Children – Print Making |
| 4542 | Crafts for Children – Making Kites |
| 4543 | Crafts for Children – Making Models |
| 4544 | Crafts for Children – Making Masks |
| 4545 | Crafts for Children – Jewelry Making |
| 4546 | Crafts for Children – Paper Crafts |
| 4547 | Walter Foster Cartooning Kits – Cartoon Animation Kit |
| 4548 | Walter Foster Cartooning Kits – U Can Cartoon! Drawing Kit |
| 4549 | Horses (How to Draw and Paint Series) |
| 4550 | Drawing Animals (How to Draw and Paint Series) |
| 4551 | Basic Animation (How to Draw and Paint Series) |
| 4552 | Cartoon Animation (How to Draw and Paint Series) |
| 4553 | Comic Strips (How to Draw and Paint Series) |
| 4554 | Creating Cartoon Characters (How to Draw and Paint Series) |
| 4555 | Creating Cartoon Animals (How to Draw and Paint Series) |
| 4556 | How to Draw #1 (How to Draw and Paint Series) |
| 4557 | How to Draw #2 (How to Draw and Paint Series) |
| 4558 | U Can Cartoon (How to Draw and Paint Series) |
| 4559 | Shapes in Outer Space (Learn and Draw Series Kit) |
| 4560 | Colors in the Rain Forest (Learn and Draw Series Kit) |
| 4561 | 1 to 10 Under the Sea (Learn and Draw Series Kit) |